Greater Than a Tourist Book Series
Reviews from Readers

I think the series is wonderful and beneficial for tourists to get information before visiting the city.

-Seckin Zumbul, Izmir Turkey

I am a world traveler who has read many trip guides but this one really made a difference for me. I would call it a heartfelt creation of a local guide expert instead of just a guide.

-Susy, Isla Holbox, Mexico

New to the area like me, this is a must have!

-Joe, Bloomington, USA

This is a good series that gets down to it when looking for things to do at your destination without having to read a novel for just a few ideas.

-Rachel, Monterey, USA

Good information to have to plan my trip to this destination.

-Pennie Farrell, Mexico

Great ideas for a port day.

-Mary Martin USA

Aptly titled, you won't just be a tourist after reading this book. You'll be greater than a tourist!

-Alan Warner, Grand Rapids, USA

Even though I only have three days to spend in San Miguel in an upcoming visit, I will use the author's suggestions to guide some of my time there. An easy read - with chapters named to guide me in directions I want to go.

 -Robert Catapano, USA

Great insights from a local perspective! Useful information and a very good value!

 -Sarah, USA

This series provides an in-depth experience through the eyes of a local. Reading these series will help you to travel the city in with confidence and it'll make your journey a unique one.

-Andrew Teoh, Ipoh, Malaysia

GREATER THAN A TOURIST- SOUTH DAKOTA

50 Travel Tips from a Local

Max Hunhoff

Cover designed by: Ivana Stamenkovic
Cover Image: https://pixabay.com/photos/deerfield-lake-south-dakota-water-3304563/

CZYK Publishing Since 2011.

Greater Than a Tourist

Lock Haven, PA

ISBN: 9781706208716

>TOURIST

50 TRAVEL TIPS FROM A LOCAL

BOOK DESCRIPTION

Are you excited about planning your next trip? Do you want to try something new? Would you like some guidance from a local? If you answered yes to any of these questions, then this Greater Than a Tourist book is for you. Greater Than a Tourist-South Dakota by Max Hunhoff offers an inside scoop on the Midwest treasure of South Dakota. Most travel books tell you how to travel like a tourist. Although there is nothing wrong with that, as part of the Greater Than a Tourist series, this book will give you travel tips from someone who has lived at your next travel destination.

In these pages, you will discover advice that will help you throughout your stay. This book will not tell you exact addresses or store hours but instead will give you excitement and knowledge from a local that you may not find in other smaller print travel books.

Travel like a local. Slow down, stay in one place, and get to know the people and culture. By the time you finish this book, you will be eager and prepared to travel to your next destination.

Inside this travel guide book you will find:

- Insider tips from a local.

- Packing and planning list.

- List of travel questions to ask yourself or others while traveling.

- A place to write your travel bucket list.

OUR STORY

Traveling is a passion of the Greater than a Tourist book series creator. Lisa studied abroad in college, and for their honeymoon Lisa and her husband toured Europe. During her travels to Malta, an older man tried to give her some advice based on his own experience living on the island since he was a young boy. She was not sure if she should talk to the stranger but was interested in his advice. When traveling to some places she was wary to talk to locals because she was afraid that they weren't being genuine. Through her travels, Lisa learned how much locals had to share with tourists. Lisa created the Greater Than a Tourist book series to help connect people with locals. A topic that locals are very passionate about sharing.

TABLE OF CONTENTS

13. Firehouse Brewing Company

14. Stage Stop Cafe

15. Tyndall Bakery

16. Meridian Corner

Rapid City

17. Prioritize

18. Badlands

19. Bear Country

20. The Caves

21. Black Elk Peak

22. Hotel Alex Johnson

23. Custer State Park

24. Hall of Records in Mount Rushmore

25. Mount Rushmore

26. Crazy Horse National Monument

Sioux Falls

27. Falls Park

28. Cathedral of Saint Joseph

29. Downtown Sioux Falls

30. Washington Pavilion

31. Butterfly House & Aquarium

32. Buffalo Ridge 1880 Cowboy Town

33. Jazzfest

Everywhere Else

34. Corn Palace

35. Wall Drug

DEDICATION

This book is dedicated to my Mom and Dad, who are lifetime South Dakotans and helped me learn to love this beautiful state.

ABOUT THE AUTHOR

Max Hunhoff was born and raised in Yankton, South Dakota and graduated from the University of South Dakota with a B.S.W in 2018. Max currently lives in Phoenix, Arizona with his wife Kristin, but the Midwest still holds a special place in his heart, specifically his home state. Max has a passion for travel and exploring strange landmarks or destinations. Max has learned many things throughout his life in South Dakota, but the one fact that remains is how much better South Dakota is than Iowa.

HOW TO USE THIS BOOK

The *Greater Than a Tourist* book series was written by someone who has lived in an area for over three months. The goal of this book is to help travelers either dream or experience different locations by providing opinions from a local. The author has made suggestions based on their own experiences. Please check before traveling to the area in case the suggested places are unavailable.

Travel Advisories: As a first step in planning any trip abroad, check the Travel Advisories for your intended destination.
https://travel.state.gov/content/travel/en/traveladvisories/traveladvisories.html

FROM THE PUBLISHER

Traveling can be one of the most important parts of a person's life. The anticipation and memories that you have are some of the best. As a publisher of the Greater Than a Tourist, as well as the popular *50 Things to Know* book series, we strive to help you learn about new places, spark your imagination, and inspire you. Wherever you are and whatever you do I wish you safe, fun, and inspiring travel.

Lisa Rusczyk Ed. D.
CZYK Publishing

WELCOME TO
> TOURIST

"For me, walking in a hard Dakota wind can be like staring at the ocean: humbled before its immensity, I also have a sense of being at home on this planet, my blood so like the sea in chemical composition, my every cell partaking of air. I live about as far from the sea as is possible in North America, yet I walk in a turbulent ocean."

- Kathleen Norris, Dakota: A Spiritual Geography

I've met a lot of individuals from various parts of the country and something I hear far too often is how South Dakota is a "flyover state." Many of the states in the Midwest have been granted this label since residents of the United States literally fly over them to travel to the coasts. Less literally, they are given this name because they are perceived to be boring and less cultured than other parts of the US.

As a life-long South Dakotan, I can safely say this perception is false. South Dakota is an amazing place full of remarkable culture, landmarks, and activities. I

11

grew up watching my peers move away, but time and time again they returned. There's something about South Dakota that you can't shake. The quote I chose isn't the most romantic, but I love how it paints a picture of a rugged, untouched place, full of history and mystery. Yet, even with those harsh descriptions, that's not how it feels to spend time here. The weather can be tough, but that just makes you marvel at those who lived here before us, and the winter chill always subsides to reveal a new season of beauty. South Dakota may not be for everyone, but after reading this book, I hope you decide to check it out.

I've broken this book up into sections. First, I discuss the best times to travel to South Dakota. I follow with some tips for first-timers to make sure they get the most out of their SoDak journey. For all my foodies, I highlight some of the best foods in the state. I finish with my suggestions for the two juggernauts, Rapid City and Sioux Falls, and lastly with the rest of South Dakota. In true South Dakotan fashion, I will also provide you multiple bonus tips at the end of the book, free of charge. I hope you enjoy this book and come away with some fun ideas for your future trip to the Mount Rushmore state.

South Dakota
United States

Pierre
South Dakota
Climate

	High	Low
January	30	10
February	35	14
March	46	24
April	60	35
May	72	47
June	82	57
July	90	63
August	89	61
September	79	51
October	63	38
November	46	25
December	33	13

GreaterThanaTourist.com

Temperatures are in Fahrenheit degrees.
Source: NOAA

TIMES TO GO:

1. COATS AND JACKETS NOT REQUIRED

So, before you decide to make the journey to South Dakota, I need to share when to come. South Dakota has a lot of activities that vary by the seasons, so timing is key. My first tip is a broad one, so I apologize in advance. Technically, South Dakotans get to experience four seasons. Realistically, we get two. Winter goes for about 9 months. The small period of time where the rain melts the snow on the ground creating a slushy disaster is "spring." The brief moment where you get to see the leaves change color and then wake up to three inches of snow is "fall." If you plan on visiting South Dakota and don't want to wear a coat or jacket of any kind, then the ONLY safe time is Mid-May to Mid-August. If you come before or after that time period, I cannot promise you will avoid chilly temperatures, snow, or a possible blizzard. Proceed with caution.

2. WINTER

Winter in South Dakota is more than a season, it's a way of life. Hunting, ice fishing, skiing, and various winter activities abound during the winter months. My personal favorite is sledding down steep hills and drinking away my injuries with hot chocolate. Christmas light drives through town are a regular family activity. I know that sounds lovely, but winter is not for the faint of heart. During Winter, parts of South Dakota will become colder than Antarctica or Siberia. In 2019 alone, multiple areas in South Dakota experienced temperatures of −60 degrees Fahrenheit (yes you read that right, negative 60). In high school, I lived about two blocks from my school. A wind chill advisory had been issued, but I decided to walk to school anyway. After walking directly into the gusts, the tears from my eyes had frozen to my face. Good times, good times. If you think you are up to the task, I wish you luck!

3. SUMMER

Despite the intense winters, South Dakota does have some beautiful summers as well. Festivals, rodeos, water activities and so much more await the summertime traveler. Many of my suggestions in this book take place in the summer or are more enjoyable during warmer months. Many campgrounds throughout the state fill up over a year in advance, so plan accordingly! The window may be a small one, but if you can make it, I promise it will be a wonderful summer experience.

WORDS OF WISDOM/WARNING:

4. IRENE

Sitting in a valley on Highway 46 is the little town of Irene. With a population of 437, it is a classic example of a small South Dakota town. If you stand in the right spot you can see through the entire town. However, what makes this place special is the ferocity of the police department towards speeding. I can't count the number of people I've met over the years who were caught in the act while driving through Irene. Even one of my high school tennis coaches was a victim of Irene's strict speed limit rules. Moral of the story, slow down through Irene.

5. DON'T BE AFRAID TO ASK FOR DIRECTIONS

I have lived in a couple places in the United States during my life, and one thing I have found to be true is the notion that people from the Midwest are the friendliest. Trust me, there is absolutely no doubt about it. If you ever find yourself lost on your South Dakota expedition, don't be afraid to ask someone for directions. I am almost certain you will be greeted warmly and likely given suggestions for other fun things to do in the area.

6. STOP AND GET SENTIMENTAL

This tip is for those who are consumed by wanderlust. South Dakota is full of incredible history, and many areas are largely untouched by the modern world. While driving through the rolling prairies, I would advise you to pull off to the side and take some time to admire a place in the world that hasn't changed in thousands of years. I promise it's a powerful experience. There are even some designated lookout points that give a vast view of the rolling fields of the prairie. I know that sounds a little odd but trust me on this.

7. DON'T AVOID THE SMALL TOWNS

Although I might have paranoid you with my warning about Irene, it's actually a lovely little town. To be honest, many of the small towns in South Dakota are amazing places full of hidden gems. Some of my favorite memories growing up took place in towns with populations under 1000. I will be referencing multiple events and restaurants in this book that most tourists would never find due to a lack of exposure. I would urge you to take a few detours. You might be surprised with what you find!

8. 80 ON THE INTERSTATE

I enjoy driving fast just as much as the next person. However, South Dakota interstates are not the place to do it. In the last few years, the speed limit on interstates was increased to 80 miles per hour. Sounds great, right? Well, it is great until you go 81 miles per hour and are slammed with a huge speeding ticket. South Dakota is one of the only states I've visited that has signs as you enter state lines stating "speed limits are firm." There is no wiggle room on the big roads, so be wary.

EAT LIKE A LOCAL

9. INCA MEXICAN RESTAURANT

I love food, and South Dakota is full of amazing culinary choices. To begin my food suggestions, I want to point you in the direction of Inca Mexican Restaurant in Sioux Falls. As someone who has traveled to southern California, Arizona, and Texas, I can safely say the food at Inca is some of the most authentic Mexican food I've ever had. Truly a wonderful place. Inca has some of the richest moles I've found in South Dakota as well. Make sure to try their fresh horchata, it's to die for.

10. PHILIPS AVENUE DINER

Also located in Sioux Falls, the Philips Avenue Diner is nestled in the trendy downtown area of the city. Designed as an old-timey diner with neon lights and bar stools at the soda counter, this diner built inside a silver airstream trailer is a blast from the past. Although the diner aims to achieve the old-timey feel, the food is far from dated. With modern spins on classic dishes, you will be glad you chose this funky little spot.

11. KEG STEAKHOUSE & BAR

In the little town of Tabor, about 20 minutes outside of Yankton, lies a little dive bar called Keg Steakhouse & Bar. A wonderful small-town atmosphere is complimented well with delicious food and a full-service bar. In the summer, if you plan your trip perfectly, you may end up going on a night they're offering $1 hamburgers. Trust me, it's a life-changing experience. If you order more than 5 hamburgers, I can't promise you won't receive some strange looks.

12. CHARLIE'S PIZZA

A nationally award-winning pizza joint, Charlie's Pizza in Yankton is a favorite of many South Dakotans. The pizzas are named after various movie stars, and they taste as show-stopping as they sound. Some crowd favorites include the Clint Eastwood, containing barbeque sauce and chicken, and the Woody Allen, covered in every vegetable imaginable. Although a bit pricey, this pizza joint is well worth it for a true South Dakotan experience.

13. FIREHOUSE BREWING COMPANY

Built inside an old firehouse in Rapid City, Firehouse Brewing Company is a pub that offers a variety of delicious options. Along with the down-to-earth menu, Firehouse also contains South Dakota's oldest operating brewery. Combine all that with live music and frequent events and you have a recipe for success. The beer battered fish tacos are unreal.

14. STAGE STOP CAFE

The town of Cheyenne Crossing started as a stagecoach stop in South Dakota's black hills. Within this tiny place is the Stage Stop Café, which makes world-famous Indian Tacos that have been featured on Food Network. They are huge and they are delicious. They serve other food too, and are open for breakfast, lunch, and supper!

15. TYNDALL BAKERY

The small town of Tyndall holds one of South Dakota's most famous bakeries. Featured in magazines, foodnetwork.com, and various other outlets, this modest bakery creates some incredible sweet treats. Some of their creations include donuts, breads, and authentic German kuchen. However, Tyndall Bakery's specialty is a Czech dessert called a kolach, and they are magical. Think fruit danish, but 200 times better.

16. MERIDIAN CORNER

Close to the town of Freeman on the corner of Highway 81 and Highway 18 is Meridan Corner, a lone building that serves South Dakota classics. This establishment is famous for chislic, a beloved South Dakota dish that consists of cubed meat grilled to perfection over an open fire. If you're feeling adventurous, you could order tiger meat, which is uncooked ground beef seasoned with spices. Definitely not my cup of tea.

RAPID CITY
17. PRIORITIZE

Growing up in South Dakota, residents were divided into two groups, East River and West River. The titles should be self-explanatory, but if you are struggling, any residents of South Dakota that lived east or west of the Missouri River were considered separate entities, bound by a fierce loyalty to their side of the state. I am east river, born and raised, so I say this with great pain; Rapid City is the best. The city, and all of the surrounding attractions and landmarks, are truly amazing. Rapid City is one of my favorite places to visit in the entire United States, but with that comes a problem. There's just too much to do. If you decide to travel to Rapid City, it is essential that you prioritize what you want to do. If you arrive without a plan, Rapid City will swallow you up and your trip will suffer because of it. Be prepared

18. BADLANDS

Badlands National Park is a 244,000 acre domain that houses striking rock formations, fossil beds, rich wildlife, and so much more. Designated as a national monument in 1929, it didn't become a national park until 1978. The park also services the nearby minuteman missile historic site. Hiking and camping are popular in this area but watch out for rattlesnakes! The rock formations themselves are made up of mostly sedimentary rock, so be careful when climbing because you could lose your footing quickly. The park can get VERY muddy when it rains so bring some hiking boots if you want to avoid getting stuck. If you're feeling adventurous, you can find helicopter rides that will take you over the park. To this day, I swear I saw a jackalope (half jackrabbit, half antelope) but no one except my mother believes me. In all seriousness, some of my most treasured childhood memories have taken place at the Badlands. I hope you have the same experience as I did.

19. BEAR COUNTRY

If you've ever felt like you wanted to be 5 feet away from a giant black bear, then this next suggestion is for you. Bear Country is an amazing attraction about 8 miles outside of Rapid City that allows visitors to see bears, elk, mountain lions, buffalo, reindeer and other wildlife in their own habitat. Please stay in your cars during the drive through the park or the exhibit might become a little too interactive. After driving through the park, make sure to check out the baby bears and other small animals located near the gift shop! They're pretty cute and are usually taking part in a bear cub fight club.

20. THE CAVES

The Rapid City area is famous for a variety of caves that draw hundreds of thousands of tourists a year. The two most famous are Jewel Cave and Wind Cave. Jewel Cave is the third longest cave in the world and was named for the incredible calcite formations on its walls. Wind Cave is one of the oldest national parks in the country and hosts some of the most intricate tunnels in the world. I am the only person in my family who hasn't experienced the caves, such is the life of a middle child. However, my family has told me that both of the caves are spectacular.

21. BLACK ELK PEAK

Black Elk Peak is the highest point in South Dakota, as well as the highest point in the United States east of the Rocky Mountains. Previously named Harney Peak, the mountain was renamed to Black Elk Peak in honor of the famous Lakota medicine man, Black Elk. The sign at the start of the 6.4-mile trail states hikers should plan for a 6-hour journey, but that is for the most leisurely of climbers. On the top of this fairly challenging hike, you'll come to an old fire lookout station that serves as wonderful place to take in the scenery. Make sure to take your time near the top, I nearly passed out on the stairs.

22. HOTEL ALEX JOHNSON

For any paranormal investigators, Hotel Alex Johnson could be the thrill you're looking for. Multiple ghosts have been spotted in the hotel over the years, including a "white woman" and Alex Johnson himself! The hotel was also featured on the SyFy television show, Ghost Hunters. I'm not a big believer in ghosts, but this hotel is still an experience to remember.

23. CUSTER STATE PARK

One of the most beautiful places in South Dakota, Custer State Park encompasses 71,000 acres of mountains, lakes, abundant wildlife, and all the recreational activities you could dream of. Custer State Park is South Dakota's first state park, as well as its largest. A selection of nine campgrounds should provide you will all the options you need to book your trip to this incredible place. Every September, there is an annual bison roundup in the park. Some of the herd are sold to make sure the number of animals is compatible for the land itself. Also, make time to find the begging burros. Introduced into the park by humans, they have become semi-feral, but still approach humans to beg for any kind of food possible. They especially like apples and will stick their head in car windows to find them.

24. HALL OF RECORDS IN MOUNT RUSHMORE

I cheated on this next selection because the general public can't actually visit the Hall of Records. Why you may ask? First, it is located behind Abraham Lincoln's head on Mount Rushmore. Second, it is sealed inside a titanium vault. Gutzon Borglum, the architect for Mount Rushmore, wanted to create a time capsule that explained why the monument was constructed, as well as provide valuable information about the United States. The original project was too complex, but 16 panels that contain US history were placed in the vault and stored away for future generations to uncover. Nicholas Cage might have something to say about that.

25. MOUNT RUSHMORE

The namesake of the state, Mount Rushmore is the famous statue depicting the four US presidents George Washington, Abraham Lincoln, Thomas Jefferson and Theodore Roosevelt. The site attracts over two million visitors every year. There's not much else to say about this location. Unfortunately, this monument was built on land that had originally been promised to the Lakota people. I am not a huge fan of this destination for that reason. That being said, the gift shop sells some pretty delicious ice cream and the rows of state flags leading up to the monument are pretty cool. The whole monument is going slightly uphill, which makes for prime photo-bombing opportunities.

26. CRAZY HORSE NATIONAL MONUMENT

Although not yet finished, the Crazy Horse National Monument is already considered the 8th wonder of the world in progress. Once completed, it would be the second tallest statue in the world. To

31

give you some perspective, the faces on Mount Rushmore are 60 feet tall, whereas the finished Crazy Horse monument is projected to be 563 feet tall. The completed monument will show the legendary figure on horseback pointing into the distance. Unfortunately, the monument has been under construction for almost 70 years and is nowhere near completion. The Indian University of North America was built nearby so students could learn more about American Indian culture while working at the monument. One of my old college professors is the director there, so I had to make sure I mentioned it!

SIOUX FALLS

27. FALLS PARK

Located in downtown Sioux Falls, Falls Park is exactly what it sounds like, a park full of waterfalls. Voted the number one attraction in Sioux Falls, it's not hard to see why so many come to see this amazing location. A lookout tower allows visitors to examine the entire park. There's also a giftshop for any souvenir junkies. In the winter months, the entire park is covered in lights and decorations, transforming into a winter wonderland! A word of warning. On breezy days, the smells from a nearby pork processing plant can invade the park, so plan accordingly.

28. CATHEDRAL OF SAINT JOSEPH

Completed in 1919, the Cathedral of Saint Joseph towers over the city of Sioux Falls. The trademark twin spires can be spotted throughout the city. One of the most beautiful pieces of architecture in the state, the cathedral was built in under 4 years, an incredible achievement of engineering. Guided and self-guided tours are available but be sure to call ahead of time. If you choose to explore the cathedral, do so respectfully.

29. DOWNTOWN SIOUX FALLS

The downtown area of Sioux Falls is a vibrant area full of shops, restaurants, attractions, and much more. A variety of monthly events add to the exciting atmosphere. The area continues to grow and flourish. Another cool aspect is how the business owners in the downtown district seem to have each other's backs. A few years ago, an old building connected to a coffee shop collapsed. After the tragedy, the support from the entire downtown community to help the affected shop was incredible. This camaraderie seeps into the soul of the area itself. The area also has the sculpture walk, a year-round outdoor exhibit of amazing sculptures that line the streets of downtown. There's always something happening in Downtown Sioux Falls, so go check it out!

30. WASHINGTON PAVILION

Housed inside the old Washington High School, the Washinton Pavilion is one of Sioux Falls' hubs for entertainment. Incredible musical acts, plays, and entertainers from around the world have performed at the pavilion. The Washinton Pavilion also contains the Kirby Science Discovery Center, three floors of scientific displays, fun activities, and a gigantic spherical theatre called the Cinedome. You can rent the giant theatre for special screenings of movies or to play video games. In fact, I hosted my bachelor party there and it was unbelievable. Also, if you've ever wanted to lift a car, then this is the place for you. No, I'm not kidding.

31. BUTTERFLY HOUSE & AQUARIUM

The Butterfly House & Aquarium is home to 800 species of butterflies and the only saltwater aquarium in South Dakota. The butterfly exhibit is one of a few in the country that is open year-round and walking into an 80-degree tropical forest feels nice in the middle of winter. Along with all the fun the butterfly house provides, they are also very involved in conservation efforts. I can't explain the feeling when a gigantic monarch butterfly lands on your shoulder and hangs out, so you'll just have to experience it for yourself. Word of advice; leave the butterflies alone and don't touch them. That will put you on a fast track out of the butterfly house.

32. BUFFALO RIDGE 1880 COWBOY TOWN

One of the creepier destinations on my list, Buffalo Ridge 1880 Cowboy Town is a bizarre wild west theme park built in the 1960s to compliment a family gas station. The "town" is full of robot citizens, many of which have fallen into disrepair. Since repairs are done sparingly, the animatronic characters are in different stages of functioning. Some have broken down altogether and have been moved to the back of certain exhibits. Also, all of the characters are voiced by the original owner. If you've ever felt the need to visit a robot ghost town, then you'll probably enjoy this strange place.

33. JAZZFEST

One of the coolest music festivals in South Dakota, Jazzfest is a free, two-day festival full of the best jazz musicians in the country. Some past headliners include Joe Walsh, Gary Clark Jr., The Fray, George Thorogood and Kenny Wayne Shepherd. The atmosphere is laid-back, and jazz aficionados are some of the kindest you'll meet. Any music lover should make attending this festival a priority!

EVERYWHERE ELSE
34. CORN PALACE

Yes, you read that right, the corn palace. Built in 1892, the "world's only corn palace" has attracted hundreds of thousands of visitors every year! Although it's not an actual palace made of corn, the unique attraction in Mitchell is decorated with murals and decorations made entirely of corn and other grains and the decorations change yearly. The current palace is actually corn palace number 3, since the first two were deemed too small for the growing success. The Corn Palace hosts sporting events, concerts, and the annual corn palace festival throughout the year.

35. WALL DRUG

Chances are, if you have driven through South Dakota or the Midwest, you have seen billboards for Wall Drug. The advertising campaign is known for its huge range, and posters for this sprawling tourist town can be found around the world. Located in the tiny town of Wall, this large collection of shops and restaurants has everything you could offer, including a gigantic animatronic dinosaur. Although many things in life aren't free, the ice water at Wall Drug actually is. They also have some pretty awesome donuts.

36. GAVINS POINT DAM

A few miles outside of Yankton, the Gavins Point Dam sprawls across the boundaries of South Dakota and Nebraska. The dam and connected power plant have tours available during the summer and on holidays. One of my first school field trips was to this dam, and the amount of improvements they've made in the last couple decades is stunning. The dam contains an enormous bomb shelter the size of a football field that was built during the Cold War. Standing above the massive turbines is also a humbling experience, so go check it out!

37. LITERALLY ANYTHING ON THE MISSOURI RIVER

The Missouri River, affectionately known as the "Mighty Mo," is the main river that flows through South Dakota. People from all over the world travel to South Dakota to spend time on the longest river in North America. Any kind of water-related activity you can think of is available on the Missouri. The river is also home to important ecological projects and many unique species call the river their home. During the summer, the river is going to be swamped with people, so get there early!

38. FRIDAY NIGHT FOOTBALL

For those of you who didn't grow up in the Midwest, high school football is almost a religious organization. Friday night football games draw out entire towns to cheer on their teams. If you want to experience some serious passion, try to attend a game and you won't be disappointed. One of my favorite stories of football devotion was when my wife was trying to find her wedding dress. She called me, annoyed, stating that she had been slightly rushed out of the store because they were closing early for, you guessed it, high school football.

39. RIVERBOAT DAYS

Every August, Yankton hosts Riverboat Days, a huge city-wide event that draws over 100,000 visitors from around the country. The three-day festival contains about any kind of entertainment you could ask for. A local couple is honored every year as the Captain and Belle of the festival, and the annual poker run has been known to draw some serious crowds. Some of my favorite activities over the years have been the nightly musical acts, the arm-wrestling tournament (which my Dad won one year) and the parade. So come check it out, buy a giant turkey leg and enjoy the sights, you won't regret it.

40. USD VS SDSU

If you enjoy sporting rivalries, then it doesn't get much better than USD vs SDSU. South Dakota's two largest universities have been competing against each other since the 1800s, and no matter the sport, the contests are fierce. As a USD graduate, I'm obviously biased in my views of the rivalry, but SDSU has dominated almost every sporting match-up. Nevertheless, it's always a lot of fun to see the two schools go head-to-head. Just to clarify, USD beat SDSU 73-6 back in 1912, the most lopsided victory in the rivalry. Go yotes!

41. NATIONAL MUSIC MUSEUM

Many would be surprised to find out the National Music Museum is in Vermillion, South Dakota. The museum contains some incredibly rare instruments, including the oldest cello in the world, which is almost 500 years old. Visitors are able to check out an MP3 device that has recordings of many of the instruments on display, and guided tours are available daily. The museum hosts concerts periodically where

41

trained musicians will play some of the rarest instruments in the collection.

42. MERIDIAN BRIDGE

A favorite of Yankton residents, the Meridan Bridge was once a fully operational double-deck bridge that connected South Dakota and Nebraska. It was eventually shut down due to old age and county officials came close to demolishing it. For a few years, the once mighty bridge stood over the river. One of my old buddies secretly climbed on the top deck while it was out of commission, but you didn't hear that from me. Anyway, the bridge was ultimately renovated and transformed into a pedestrian walking bridge. Today, the bridge hosts various dining and art events, as well as races. A small park and splash pad was also installed at the base of the bridge. The Meridian Bridge is now the pride and joy of the community of Yankton.

43. DIGNITY

Dignity is a large sculpture in the town of Chamberlain that depicts an indigenous woman in traditional plains-style dress holding up a quilt. The statue was dedicated to the Lakota and Dakota people, who lived in the South Dakota area for thousands of years prior to colonization. The statue was created by South Dakota artist laureate Dale Lamphere along with a team of other sculptors, an automotive paint specialist, and an engineering company which ensured the statue would withstand the harsh winds. The statue is 50 feet tall and the quilt has 100 blue diamond shapes that move in the wind. Standing on top of a hill overlooking the river, the statue is a beautiful testament to the strength and courage of indigenous people.

44. SOUTH DAKOTA TRACTOR MUSEUM

The town of Kimball is home to the South Dakota Tractor Museum. The large series of warehouses contains tractors, farm equipment, and various artifacts that hold significance for life on the prairie. Volunteers of the museum also recreated an authentic one-room schoolhouse that was painstakingly moved from a different location piece by piece. The museum also has a fully functioning blacksmith shop!

45. OKATON GHOST TOWN

Close to Murdo, the Okaton Ghost Town started as a railroad town, but the harsh weather and lack of railroad usage in the area caused many residents to leave. What makes this ghost town unique is its history. A family named the Westlakes thought they could revitalize the town by transforming it into a tourist attraction, complete with petting zoo and a general store. However, they too moved on and presently, the community is almost abandoned.

46. HUGH GLASS MEMORIAL

The Hugh Glass Memorial can be found outside of Lemmon and is a monument for one of the most amazing men in South Dakota history. Hugh Glass, the subject of the 2015 film "The Revenant," was a trapper who fought off a grizzly bear attack. After the attack, Glass crawled over 200 miles before finally making it to safety. This memorial honors one of the toughest frontiersman to ever live. And to think, I was just about to complain to myself about a headache.

47. SPIRIT MOUND

Outside of Vermillion, Spirit Mound is a prominent hill that Plains Indians believed was the home of dangerous spirits. Lewis and Clark themselves climbed the hill during their expedition. The state park was officially established in 2001 with an emphasis on prairie restoration. However, there is some controversy surrounding Spirit Mound and its establishment as a state park. For many indigenous people, the hill is seen as a terrifying place, and many local tribes were shocked that it was being transformed into a leisurely attraction.

48. DAKOTA DAYS

The University of South Dakota's homecoming festivities, Dakota Days (or D-Days), is a week-long celebration in Vermillion. If you're a fan of partying, then this is the place to be. D-Days has become infamous for its wild parties, and the town hunkers down every year for the onslaught. Not everything is crazy though. A parade is held throughout the town and Vermillion really comes alive. I do have to come clean when I say I never actually participated in any of the "festivities." That being said, if you want to see a LARGE collection of drunk people, then this is your best bet.

49. THE ICEHOUSE

The first artificial ice plant in the area, the Icehouse has been transformed into a dive bar in Yankton. Shortly after prohibition, the Icehouse began selling alcohol. The quirky business serves beer out on the old loading dock of the plant, and patrons simply toss their empty bottles under the deck when they're finished. Breaking a bottle on the old brick wall has become a trademark. The Icehouse is such a staple of the community that you will regularly see wedding photos being taken on the dock. It is also one of the only bars in the country with "carhop" service.

50. RODEOS

I would be amiss if I didn't include rodeos in a book about South Dakota travel tips. Rodeos are a huge part of South Dakota culture. In fact, one of the recent gubernatorial candidates, Billie Sutton, was a rodeo star before a tragic accident left him paralyzed from the waist down. There are dozens of rodeos throughout the summer hosted by communities large and small, so finding one to attend shouldn't be too difficult. In fact, the state sport of South Dakota is rodeo.

BONUS TIPS*

* 4th of July Fireworks in Yankton

The city of Yankton hosts one of the most impressive fireworks displays in the state during the 4th of July. The fireworks are launched off the top of the Meridian Bridge and reflect off the waters of the Missouri River below. The display is coordinated by a huge group of volunteers and the city fire department stands guard in case anything should go wrong. The grand finale is always jaw-dropping. Make sure to bring bug spray since mosquitoes can be annoying that close to the water.

* Mount Moriah Cemetery

This cemetery in Deadwood contains the graves of legendary wild west figures like Wild Bill Hickok and Calamity Jane. Although some people might find visiting a graveyard eerie, the amount of history in this facility is second to none. The late-Victorian cemetery has paved roads which make exploring easy while also being respectful. The visitor center contains an educational movie and instructional panels so you can learn more about the cemetery.

There's also death statistics for Deadwood, which was a wild town back in the day!

- Needles Highway

Deemed the "impossible highway" by critics, Needles Highway was constructed in 1922. One of the most stunning drives in the country, the national scenic byway is a white-knuckle journey through the black hills in Custer State Park. Probably not a great idea if you're afraid of heights, these winding roads take you on an uncomfortably close journey to the edge of mountain sides and through narrow tunnels.

- Deadwood

Founded in 1876 shortly after the great gold rush in the Black Hills, Deadwood was named after the gulch full of dead trees where the town was ultimately built. The famous old-west town where Wild Bill Hickok was famously shot has transformed into a tourist destination over the years. Casinos, saloons, and historical reenactments make this a vibrant place to visit. The town was also the setting of the HBO tv series "Deadwood." If you choose to gamble, please play responsibly.

- Sturgis Motorcycle Rally

Starting in 1937, the world-famous Sturgis Motorcycle Rally draws a crowd of over 500,000 riders from around the United States. The ten-day festival has musicians, food, and various events to keep bikers happy. The rally can get fairly hectic, so stay vigilant! Hotels throughout the area sell out months in advance, with open rooms costing thousands of dollars in some locations. Riding into the sunset is nice and all, but make sure to plan ahead for this monstrous event.

- Keystone

An eclectic little tourist town nestled a few miles from Mount Rushmore, Keystone has every kind of souvenir you could desire. Pizza shops, ice cream, and the BEST saltwater taffy in the universe await your taste buds. There are also chainsaw carving exhibitions and the occasional costumed street performer. There's also an old-school 1880s train that you can ride on through the valley.

- Minuteman Missile National Historic Site

Near Philip, a nuclear missile launch site developed during the Cold War still stands. This site contains the last remaining Minuteman II ICBM system in the United States. One of over 1,000 hidden in the great plains, a ballistic missile was kept on high alert for years. In 1990, the nuclear missile was removed, and an unarmed missile was placed underground instead for educational purposes. Today, the site stands as a reminder of the dangers of nuclear war and the significance of the nuclear arms race.

- Dinosaur Park

On top of a hill in Rapid City stands seven large concrete dinosaurs. Built in 1936, the depictions of the dinosaurs are pretty strange. All of the giant green creatures have googly eyes and large smiles, making for a scientifically inaccurate journey back in time. However, these dinos were built to last and have remained unchanged since being built. Free of charge, patrons are allowed to climb on the dinosaurs and take pictures next to their Jurassic friends. Don't worry, there's also a gift shop.

- Mammoth Site

Located in Hot Springs, the title is self-explanatory. The world's largest mammoth research facility, this area is an active paleontological excavation site with the largest concentration of mammoth remains in the world. The remains of over 61 mammoths have been found so far. If you'd like to see some amazing history and watch an archeological dig in progress, this might be worth a stop.

- Reptile Gardens

Located in Rapid City, Reptile Gardens has a bunch of reptiles. I know that description is underwhelming, but I can't explain it any other way. You can see some 100-year-old tortoises, alligators, and poisonous snakes. They also have birds if that's more your style. The gardens haven't always been a wonderful place. My parents told me a story about one of their old attractions. After inserting a quarter, a cage full of chickens would be forced to "dance" when electric currents were sent through the metal plates on the ground. Thankfully, over the years, the establishment has become more humane and treats their animals very well.

- Tornado Alley

If you choose to visit South Dakota during the summer, be aware that much of the state is part of the infamous "Tornado Alley." South Dakota has been home to some of the fiercest tornados in US history. In 1965, an F5 tornado as wide as 17 football fields touched down near Tripp, SD. Thankfully, that is the only F5 to ever hit South Dakota. If you find yourself on the road with a tornado nearby, find the nearest bridge or valley to hunker down in. Do not try to outrun a twister! Save that for the storm chasers.

- Wounded Knee Memorial

Wounded Knee, located on the Pine Ridge Indian Reservation, is the site of one of the darkest events in US History. In 1890, almost 200 innocent Sioux Indians were slaughtered by American soldiers. After the massacre, 20 of the soldiers were awarded the Medal of Honor. Those awards still stand, even with petitions to have them rescinded. In 1990, both houses of Congress passed a resolution stating "deep regret" for the travesty. The memorial serves as a painful reminder of the many travesties committed against indigenous people. The Wounded Knee

Museum in Wall is a good option for those who wish to learn more about the tragedy.

- Country Apple Orchard

Outside of Harrisburg, Country Apple Orchard is the perfect Fall destination. The 78-acre apple orchard takes guests out on a tractor where they are free to pick as many apples as their heart desires. Along with a pumpkin patch and gift shop selling homemade treats, this orchard is a wonderful addition to any trip. Make sure to check their website for the dates of different festivals!

- Hippie Hole

Hippie Hole is a small swimming area close to Keystone that is accessible via a hiking trail. The location is infamous for being difficult to find, but there are plenty of websites with directions to the peaceful swimming hole. Although the hike is challenging, it is well worth it. Did I mention there's also a waterfall?

- Redlin Art Center

Built in honor of famous South Dakota artist, Terry Redlin, the Redlin Art Center in Watertown is host to over 150 of the artist's original works. Open year-round, the center hosts tours daily and admission is free. There's also a sketch room that shows some of the artist's earliest renditions of paintings, which is truly fascinating. My mom even owned a Terry Redlin painting that hung in our living room my entire childhood.

- Ope

If you hear this trademark Midwest saying, someone probably came very close to running into you. That will likely be followed by "can I squeeze right past ya."

- Crash Course

Soda is called pop. Puppy chow is chex cereal covered in chocolate, peanut butter, and powdered sugar. A coney dog is a hot dog covered in tavern meat. Sneakers are just called tennis shoes, even if you don't play tennis. Shorts weather is anything above 50 degrees for the weakest South Dakotans. Cornhole is bean bag toss. Cinnamon rolls need to be eaten with chili to be enjoyed fully.

- Help spread the news

I have genuinely had conversations with people who believed residents in South Dakota still traveled around in horse-drawn wagons. I have been questioned whether my hometown had electricity. When I told one of my old co-workers from Seattle that I grew up in South Dakota, he replied, "Oh, so you're from the middle coast?" Not exactly.

All of these quotes serve to highlight one fact; people are clueless about the Midwest. So, do me a favor and explain to your east and west coast friends that South Dakotans are not hundreds of years behind like many believe. I would greatly appreciate it.

TOP REASONS TO BOOK THIS TRIP

Hospitality: While you're in South Dakota, you will be treated like family and you'll want to come back over and over again, that's a promise. I have so many stories about unplanned acts of kindness that I could have filled this book with those stories alone. The notion that midwestern people are friendlier is not a myth.

Beauty: South Dakota is one of the most beautiful places in the country, and so much of the state has went unchanged for thousands of years. At night, you can glimpse parts of the milky way galaxy thanks to the pristine skies and lack of light pollution. There's a reason so many directors have picked South Dakota as the backdrop for their films, including Dances with Wolves and Armageddon.

Midwest is Best: Traveling in South Dakota is as relaxing as it is fun. You won't have to worry about bumper to bumper traffic or air pollution warnings. Everything runs a little bit slower in South Dakota, and that means you'll have time for a little more fun! In a recent study by MagnifyMoney, South Dakota was ranked the second happiest state in the US.

One Last Thought: I'd like to leave you with one last thought about my home state and why it's such a special place. It was written by South Dakota's first poet laureate, Badger Clark. I think it sums up perfectly what it means to be a South Dakotan. The poem is titled "Fifty Years in South Dakota."

We lack sophistication; our lives are all frustration,
We South Dakotans, so some writers say
According to those novels we mostly live in hovels
And all our days are dun and gray.
We flounder in futility, punch-drunk to imbecility
From dust and debt and drought and dying kine,
Aridity, frigidity — yet I, in my stupidity
Have lived here fifty years and like it fine.
I nearly froze my gizzard in one riproaring blizzard,
But that was in the year of Eighty-eight.
Thought I was never wealthy I've been absurdly
    healthy
Like nearly all people in the state.
If skies went dry and coppery, if fields got all
    grasshoppery,
That made the good years better when 'twas done,
And though my weak humanity slipped sometimes
    to profanity
I've lived here fifty years and think it's fun.

I wonder if the fellows who paint us all in yellows
Have heard the meadowlarks among the grass
Or seen the corn in tassel or climbed a granite castle
That stands on guard above a Black Hills pass.
We like a fat prosperity but there's a tougher verity
That roots us to the prairies and the Hills.
It's HOME to us, our motherland, dearer than any
    other land,
I've lived here fifty years, but yet that thrills.
It never is "verboten" for any South Dakotan
To laugh and talk as freely as he votes,
And if they haven't riches to carry in their breeches
They always carry laughter in their throats.
Our maidens sweet and willowy, our matrons good
    and pillowy,
Our boys and men look you in the eye
Make up a grand fraternity to do me till eternity.
I've lived here fifty years, and here I'll die.

PACKING AND PLANNING TIPS

A Week before Leaving

- Arrange for someone to take care of pets and water plants.

- Email and Print important Documents.

- Get Visa and vaccines if needed.

- Check for travel warnings.

- Stop mail and newspaper.

- Notify Credit Card companies where you are going.

- Passports and photo identification is up to date.

- Pay bills.

- Copy important items and download travel Apps.

- Start collecting small bills for tips.

- Have post office hold mail while you are away.

- Check weather for the week.

- Car inspected, oil is changed, and tires have the correct pressure.

- Check airline luggage restrictions.

- Download Apps needed for your trip.

Right Before Leaving

- Contact bank and credit cards to tell them your location.

- Clean out refrigerator.

- Empty garbage cans.

- Lock windows.

- Make sure you have the proper identification with you.

- Bring cash for tips.

- Remember travel documents.

- Lock door behind you.

- Remember wallet.

- Unplug items in house and pack chargers.

- Change your thermostat settings.

- Charge electronics, and prepare camera memory cards.

READ OTHER
GREATER THAN A TOURIST
BOOKS

Greater Than a Tourist- Geneva Switzerland: 50 Travel Tips from a Local by Amalia Kartika

Greater Than a Tourist- St. Croix US Birgin Islands USA: 50 Travel Tips from a Local by Tracy Birdsall

Greater Than a Tourist- San Juan Puerto Rico: 50 Travel Tips from a Local by Melissa Tait

Greater Than a Tourist – Lake George Area New York USA: 50 Travel Tips from a Local by Janine Hirschklau

Greater Than a Tourist – Monterey California United States: 50 Travel Tips from a Local by Katie Begley

Greater Than a Tourist – Chanai Crete Greece: 50 Travel Tips from a Local by Dimitra Papagrigoraki

Greater Than a Tourist – The Garden Route Western Cape Province South Africa: 50 Travel Tips from a Local by Li-Anne McGregor van Aardt

Greater Than a Tourist – Sevilla Andalusia Spain: 50 Travel Tips from a Local by Gabi Gazon

Children's Book: *Charlie the Cavalier Travels the World* by Lisa Rusczyk Ed. D.

65

> TOURIST

Follow us on Instagram for beautiful travel images:
http://Instagram.com/GreaterThanATourist

Follow *Greater Than a Tourist* on Amazon.
>Tourist Podcast
>T Website
>T Youtube
>T Facebook
>T TikTok
>T Goodreads
>T Amazon
>T Mailing List
>T Pinterest
>T Instagram
>T Twitter
>T SoundCloud
>T LinkedIn
>T Map

> TOURIST

At *Greater Than a Tourist*, we love to share travel tips with you. How did we do? What guidance do you have for how we can give you better advice for your next trip? Please send your feedback to GreaterThanaTourist@gmail.com as we continue to improve the series. We appreciate your constructive feedback. Thank you.

METRIC CONVERSIONS

TEMPERATURE

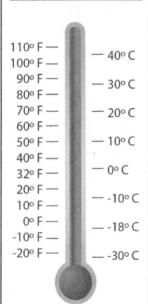

110° F	40° C
100° F	
90° F	30° C
80° F	
70° F	20° C
60° F	
50° F	10° C
40° F	
32° F	0° C
20° F	
10° F	-10° C
0° F	-18° C
-10° F	
-20° F	-30° C

To convert F to C:

Subtract 32, and then multiply
by 5/9 or .5555.

To Convert C to F:

Multiply by 1.8
and then add 32.

32F = 0C

LIQUID VOLUME

To Convert:....................Multiply by
U.S. Gallons to Liters................ 3.8
U.S. Liters to Gallons 26
Imperial Gallons to U.S. Gallons 1.2
Imperial Gallons to Liters....... 4.55
Liters to Imperial Gallons 22
1 Liter = .26 U.S. Gallon
1 U.S. Gallon = 3.8 Liters

DISTANCE

To convert ....Multiply by
Inches to Centimeters 2.54
Centimeters to Inches 39
Feet to Meters...................... .3
Meters to Feet 3.28
Yards to Meters 91
Meters to Yards 1.09
Miles to Kilometers 1.61
Kilometers to Miles............ .62
1 Mile = 1.6 km
1 km = .62 Miles

WEIGHT

1 Ounce = .28 Grams
1 Pound = .4555 Kilograms
1 Gram = .04 Ounce
1 Kilogram = 2.2 Pounds

TRAVEL QUESTIONS

- Do you bring presents home to family or friends after a vacation?

- Do you get motion sick?

- Do you have a favorite billboard?

- Do you know what to do if there is a flat tire?

- Do you like a sun roof open?

- Do you like to eat in the car?

- Do you like to wear sun glasses in the car?

- Do you like toppings on your ice cream?

- Do you use public bathrooms?

- Did you bring a cell phone and does it have power?

- Do you have a form of identification with you?

- Have you ever been pulled over by a cop?

- Have you ever given money to a stranger on a road trip?

- Have you ever taken a road trip with animals?

- Have you ever gone on a vacation alone?

- Have you ever run out of gas?

- If you could move to any place in the world, where would it be?

- If you could travel anywhere in the world, where would you travel?

- If you could travel in any vehicle, which one would it be?

- If you had three things to wish for from a magic genie, what would they be?

- If you have a driver's license, how many times did it take you to pass the test?

- What are you the most afraid of on vacation?

- What do you want to get away from the most when you are on vacation?

- What foods smell bad to you?

- What item do you bring on ever trip with you away from home?

- What makes you sleepy?

- What song would you love to hear on the radio when you're cruising on the highway?

- What travel job would you want the least?

- What will you miss most while you are away from home?

- What is something you always wanted to try?

- What is the best road side attraction that you ever saw?

- What is the farthest distance you ever biked?

- What is the farthest distance you ever walked?

- What is the weirdest thing you needed to buy while on vacation?

- What is your favorite candy?

- What is your favorite color car?

- What is your favorite family vacation?

- What is your favorite food?

- What is your favorite gas station drink or food?

- What is your favorite license plate design?

- What is your favorite restaurant?

- What is your favorite smell?

- What is your favorite song?

- What is your favorite sound that nature makes?

- What is your favorite thing to bring home from a vacation?

- What is your favorite vacation with friends?

- What is your favorite way to relax?

- Where is the farthest place you ever traveled in a car?

- Where is the farthest place you ever went North, South, East and West?

- Where is your favorite place in the world?

- Who is your favorite singer?

- Who taught you how to drive?

- Who will you miss the most while you are away?

- Who if the first person you will contact when you get to your destination?

- Who brought you on your first vacation?

- Who likes to travel the most in your life?

- Would you rather be hot or cold?

- Would you rather drive above, below, or at the speed limited?

- Would you rather drive on a highway or a back road?

- Would you rather go on a train or a boat?

- Would you rather go to the beach or the woods?

TRAVEL BUCKET LIST

1.

2.

3.

4.

5.

6.

7.

8.

9.

10.

NOTES

Made in the USA
Coppell, TX
11 November 2021

65580954R00059